Just Beyond Reach

and Other Riddle Poems

by Bonnie Larkin Nims
photographs by George Ancona

SCHOLASTIC
HARDCOVER

S C H O L A S T I C   I N C.   •   N E W   Y O R K

Library of Congress Cataloging-in-Publication Data

Nims, Bonnie Larkin.
  Just beyond reach and other riddle poems / by Bonnie Larkin
Nims; photographs by George Ancona.
      p. cm.
  Summary: Fourteen short poems provide riddles for the reader
to solve.
  ISBN 0-590-44077-2
  1. Riddles, Juvenile. 2. Children's poetry. [1. Riddles.
2. American poetry.] I. Ancona, George, ill. II. Title.
PN6371.5.N56   1992
811'.54 — dc20   91-15233
                                                      CIP
                                                       AC

12 11 10 9 8 7 6 5 4 3 2 1   2 3 4 5 6/9

Printed in the U.S.A.   36

First Scholastic printing, May 1992

Text design by Laurie McBarnette

1

A neat little room
with a big heavy door,
and a ceiling that sinks
down into the floor!

And a floor that rises
from bottom to top
till it reaches the place
where it comes to a stop.

An elevator

2

WHEW!
I'm here
to tell you
those
nothing-
looking
little
black
specks
pack
a wallop.
Bang
firecrackers
on your tongue!
BOOM cannons
through your nose!

Black pepper

3

You never close your eye.
You never sleep,
never even wink!
You just look and look,
show and show,
but never tell me
what you think.

A mirror

4

It has no taste, no tongue,
no teeth, no bite.
What it does have
is an APPETITE!
Just everything's
its favorite food —
pennies, pebbles, crumbs,
gum that's new, gum that's chewed,
keys, shells,
lots of fuzz,
bottle tops, rubber bands,
sticky candy,
an ice-cold hand —
yes, an *ice-cold* hand!

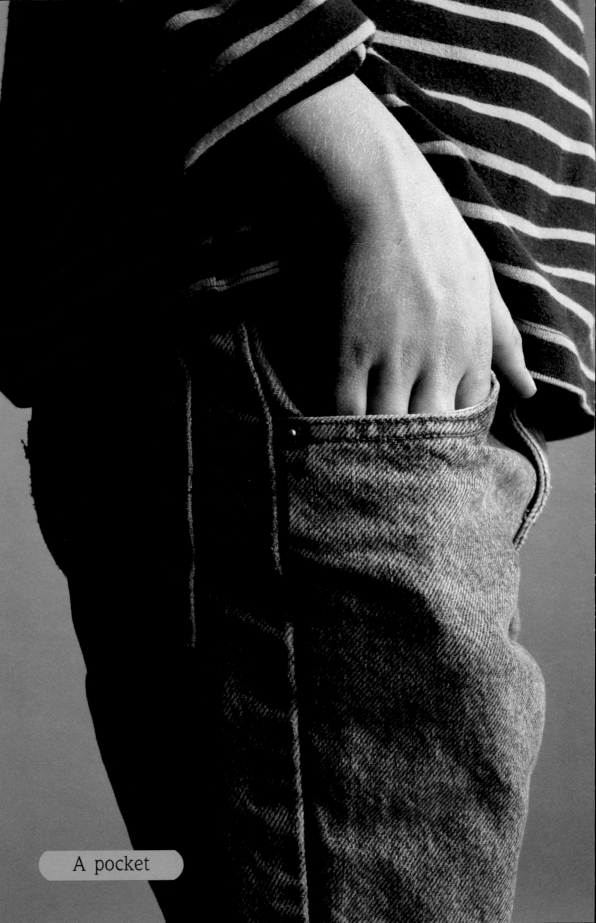

A pocket

5

It draws a line
across the air
and makes a place
that was not there.

It turns a nothing
into a street
where opposite ends
can easily meet.

It never takes sides.
It's always in the middle.
(And you'll be glad that it is
when you know this riddle!)

A bridge

6

A little bird
with a long sharp beak
and shorty legs.
Its feet are
two big zeros.
And no feathers.
Its wings
are my fingers.
Together,
we can fly
anywhere
through cloth,
paper, grass.
But never
through sky.

Scissors

7

Pink as a peach,
just beyond reach.

Purple as a plum,
on a giant's thumb.

Red as a cherry,
bobbing and merry.

Yellow as a pear,
best at the fair.

Blue as a blueberry,
not juicy, but airy.

Balloons

8

A stubby,
rubbery
tip of a tongue
licks up
letters and numbers
I got wrong,
makes my paper
look like new.

(I wish it could tell me
the right answer, too!)

An eraser

9

It's something we take
wherever we go,
no matter how far
or fast or slow.

It gets very dark
when the sun's very bright.
It's too long, too short,
or fits just right.

One for a tinker,
one for a tailor,
one for a cowboy,
one for a sailor.

Every rooster has one.
Every scooter has one.
A hat has, even a *gnat* has!
It — alone — has none.

A shadow

10

I just stopped to see
how his furry tail curled
soft as smoke,
his sleek head bent
over the seed
in his toy paw.

Then he looked up
and mostly flew
to the top
of the nearest tree.

I wonder:
Why is anyone
so quick
scared off
by a slow-
poke
like me?

A squirrel

11

Someone
or something
slipped out
from under
the inside
of a hug.
And now
there's nothing.
Just *nothing*.

A hole

12

"Like fat snowflakes," said David.
"Like real little clouds," said Pam.
"Or ghosts —" said Sally.
"Monsters from outer space!" giggled Sam.
"Blossoms falling off a tree," said Sophie.

"You guys talk so silly!"
said bad, bad Billy.
"What it looks like to me
is something I'M GONNA EAT!"

?

Popcorn

13

I found a little roof,
sitting on a stone.
It had no walls, no floor,
no windows, no door.
I was just about to give it a pat,
poor little roof,
all alone —
OUCH!
when I learned
that a roof without a house
could be a roof with someone
home.

A turtle

14

up there then it

it's slips

until away

and builds down

builds under.

that I

stair wonder

square where?

sharp ?

a ?

An escalator